Viola

More String Time Joggers

17 pieces for flexible ensemble

Kathy and David Blackwell

Contents

Illustrations by Martin Remphry

Full performances and backing tracks for all pieces are available to download from the *More String Time Joggers* Companion Website: www.oup.com/morestj

MUSIC DEPARTMENT

OXFORD
UNIVERSITY PRESS

Space Suite

1. March of the astronauts

KB & DB

Printed in Great Britain

OXFORD UNIVERSITY PRESS, MUSIC DEPARTMENT, GREAT CLARENDON STREET, OXFORD OX2 6DP

2. Lost in space

KB & DB

3. Return to Earth

Words and music by
KB & DB

We've been in ou-ter space, meet-in' an a-lien race,

But now we're com-in' back home from a-far. We've been a-way to Mars,

travel-lin' to dis-tant stars, But now we're com-in' back home, yes we are!

Speed-ing through the dark-ness in the Milk-y Way, we've Seen a-maz-ing things a-round our ga - la - xy, so Now we feel the pull from Earth and gra - vi - ty, let's fly home,

oh   yeah!_   As - te - roids and sa - tel - lites, we've seen them all,   and

Did you know the sun is like a big red ball? so Now we feel the pull from Earth and

gra - vi - ty, let's fly home,   oh   yeah!

B _f_

Thou-sands of miles we've roamed, now we are head-in' home, Good-bye to ga-la-xies

light-years a - way. In - to the ro-cket ship, time now to end our trip,

C _mp_

Hel - lo to pla-net Earth, we're on our way. Ve - nus and Mer-cu - ry,

cresc. _mf_

Nep-tune and Ju - pi - ter, Sa-turn and Ur - an - us, Plu - to and Mars,

_f_

Pla-nets both big and small, you bet we've seen them all, In all the un - i - verse we're su-per-stars! We've been in ou-ter space, meet-in' an a-lien race,

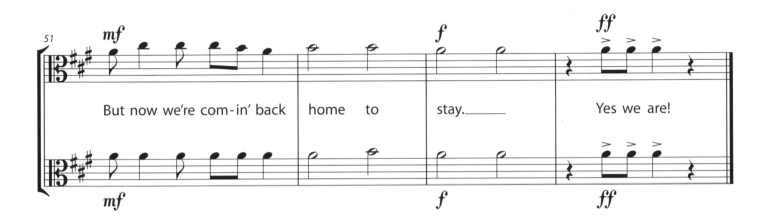

But now we're com-in' back home to stay._____ Yes we are!

Travel Suite

4. Riding my bike!

Words and music by
KB & DB

PART 1

Lively pedal-power ♩ = 112

Cycl-ing in the town I go I'm some-times fast and some-times slow I

love to pe - dal to and fro, I'm Rid-ing my bike! Cycl-ing in the coun-try-side It

real-ly is a love-ly ride To pe-dal free-ly far and wide, I'm Rid-ing my bike!

[A] Cycl - ing in the ve - lo - drome My bike is red with shi - ny chrome I'll

soon be cycl-ing off to home, I'm Rid-ing my bike! Wind and rain or sun and shower I'll

keep on cycl-ing hour by hour Be-cause I've got my pe-dal-power, I'm Rid-ing my bike!

[B] Care-ful of the lor-ries and don't get in their way, Then no-bo-dy wor-ries as you

cy - cle each day. Care-ful of the bus-es as they crawl up the street,

[C] Then no-bo-dy fus-ses as you pe-dal so neat! Cycl-ing's fun and ve-ry green It keeps the pla - net nice and clean It makes you fit and ve - ry lean, I'm

Rid-ing my bike! Up the road and down the lane Then up the hill and down a-gain It's

bet-ter than a car or plane, I'm Rid-ing my bike! Cycl-ing is the great-est thing It

makes you smile and want to sing, I'm off, Rid-ing my bike!

PART 2

Lively pedal-power ♩ = 112

Rid-ing my bike!

5. Sailing home

KB & DB

6. We're all going on an aeroplane!

KB & DB

At a flying speed ♩ = 112–120

We're all go – ing on an ae – ro – plane!

Ae – ro – plane, ae – ro – plane!

Globe-trotting Suite

7. Japanese celebration (Mura matsuri)

Japanese trad.
arr. KB & DB

8. African song (Mweya m'tsvene)

Shona trad., Zimbabwe
arr. KB & DB

9. American adventure

American trad.
arr. KB & DB

Theme Park Suite

10. Ghost train

KB & DB

Spookily ♩ = 88

A **Fast** ♩ = 126

11. Big Wheel waltz

KB & DB

Gently circling ♩ = 100

Big Wheel! *

Big Wheel! *

* In the rests in section [A] make a circle in the air with the bow, like a Big Wheel!

OPTIONAL HARMONY PART

Gently circling ♩ = 100

* In the rests in section A make a circle in the air with the bow, like a Big Wheel!

12. Rock 'n' rollercoaster

Words and music by
KB & DB

Step a-board, get

read-y to rock, rol-ler-coast-er ride! Step a-board, get read-y to rock,

we'll be side by side. Step a-board the rol-ler-coast-er ride!

Up and down, we're feel-in' diz-zy on the rol-ler-coast-er ride, Climb-in' high we'll touch the sky, we're spin-nin' so far from the ground. Step a-board the rol-ler-coast-er

ride!

Twist and turn, time to rock and roll,

rol-ler-coast-er ride!

Dip and dive, time to rock and roll,

Rol-ler-coast-er ride!

Step a-board the

rol-ler-coast-er ride!

Step a-board the rol-ler-coast-er ride!

Step a-board the rol-ler-coast-er ride, it's rock-in'!

Extras

13. Ev'ry time

Jamaican trad.
arr. and with words by KB & DB

MELODY

Ev -'ry time_ I play on my vio - la, makes me have_ a good time.

Ev - 'ry time_ I play on my cel - lo, makes me have_ a good time.

14. Slovenian folk song (Kadar boš na rajžo šel)

Slovenian trad.
arr. KB & DB

Rounds

15. Carnival time

MELODY

KB & DB

OSTINATO

16. Lotus flower

KB & DB

17. Chase!

KB & DB